W9-ARJ-072

NEWMARKET PUBLIC LIBRARY

DISCARD
NEWMARKET PUBLIC LIBRARY

NEWMARKET PUBLIC LIBRARY

# REMARKABLE CANADIANS

# Nellie McClung

## by Bryan Pezzi

Published by Weigl Educational Publishers Limited
6325 – 10 Street SE
Calgary, Alberta, Canada
T2H 2Z9

Website: www.weigl.com

Copyright ©2008 WEIGL EDUCATIONAL PUBLISHERS LIMITED
All rights reserved. No part of this publication may be reproduced, stored in a
retrieval system, or transmitted in any form or by any means, electronic, mechanical,
photocopying, recording, or otherwise, without the prior written permission of
the publisher.

All of the Internet URLs given in the book were valid at the time of publication.
However, due to the dynamic nature of the Internet, some addresses may have changed,
or sites may have ceased to exist since publication. While the author and publisher
regret any inconvenience this may cause readers, no responsibility for any such changes
can be accepted by either the author or the publisher.

Library and Archives Canada Cataloguing in Publication

Pezzi, Bryan
          Nellie McClung / Bryan Pezzi.


(Remarkable Canadians)
ISBN 978-1-55388-315-9 (bound).--ISBN 978-1-55388-316-6 (pbk.)

1. McClung, Nellie L., 1873-1951--Juvenile literature.
2. Feminists--Canada--Biography--Juvenile literature.
3. Authors, Canadian (English)--20th century--Biography--
Juvenile literature.  I. Title.  II. Series.


HQ1455.M3P49 2007          j305.42092          C2007-900889-5


Printed in the United States of America
1 2 3 4 5 6 7 8 9 0  11 10 09 08 07

Editor: Liz Brown
Design: Terry Paulhus

We acknowledge the financial support of the Government of Canada through the Book
Publishing Industry Development Program (BPIDP) for our publishing activities.

Cover: Nellie McClung worked hard to promote women's rights in Canada.

Photograph Credits
Cover: Archives of Canada (PA-030212); Archives of Canada page 13 top left; British
Columbia Archives: page 4 (b_06794), pages 10 (e_05182), 16 (g_04011), 19
(b_06788); Courtesy of Dell Mooney: pages 6, 8, 9; Courtesy of Helen Siemens: page 12;
Glenbow Archives: pages 1 (NA-273-2), 13 top right (NA-4035-138), 13 bottom left
(NA-273-1), 13 bottom right (NA-1731-3), 18 (NA-3043-1), 20 (NA-3230-1); Manitoba
Archives: pages 15, 17; Province of Manitoba: page 7 top left.

Every reasonable effort has been made to trace ownership and to obtain permission
to reprint copyright material. The publishers would be pleased to have any errors
or omissions brought to their attention so that they may be corrected in
subsequent printings.

# Contents

NEWMARKET PUBLIC LIBRARY

# Who Is Nellie McClung?

Nellie McClung was a writer, speaker, **activist**, and **politician**. She lived during a time when women did not have the same rights as men. Women in Canada could not vote in elections, and they could not work in the **Senate**. Nellie did not think this was fair. She worked hard to change the laws in Canada so that women would have the same rights as men. Nellie McClung was a woman with opinions and ideas. She felt strongly about issues affecting women. Nellie's passion and enthusiasm helped her succeed in many careers. Nellie was a leader and an inspiration to many Canadians.

> *"Never retract, never explain, never apologize—get the thing done and let them howl."*

# Growing Up

Nellie Mooney was born in Ontario in 1873. Her family moved to Manitoba's Souris Valley when she was seven years old. Nellie came from a farming family. As a young girl, she had to work on the farm with her family. Nellie began school when she was 10 years old. She was an excellent student.

Nellie's mother and father had **traditional** views. They thought that it was a woman's duty to serve her husband. Nellie had her own ideas. At town picnics, girls were not allowed to run races or play baseball. Nellie wanted to know why. She was told girls could not play sports because they wore skirts. Nellie did not think this was fair. She asked many questions, but she was told to be quiet. At age 15, Nellie decided to become a schoolteacher. She believed that she would have the power to do things differently as a teacher.

Nellie was born on a farm near Chatsworth, Ontario.

# Manitoba Tidbits

**COAT OF ARMS**

**BIRD**
Great Gray Owl

**FLOWER**
Prairie Crocus

Manitoba was the fifth province to enter **Confederation**.

The white spruce is Manitoba's provincial tree.

Manitoba's provincial motto is "glorious and free."

Winnipeg is the capital of Manitoba. It is the coldest major city in Canada.

More than one million people live in Manitoba.

## Think about it!

Nellie lived in Manitoba from 1880 to 1915. She was involved with many social issues there. Research Manitoba's history. What problems did Manitoba women face during Nellie's time? How do you think these problems influenced Nellie?

# Practice Makes Perfect

When Nellie was 16 years old, she earned her teaching certificate. This allowed her to teach school. Her first job was in a small town named Somerset. Somerset is in Manitoba. Nellie taught in a one-room schoolhouse. Sometimes, she would play sports with her students at recess. Some parents thought this was strange behaviour for a female schoolteacher.

🍁 Teachers in the 1800s, including Nellie, had to teach many different grades of students in the same classroom.

In 1892, Nellie took a teaching job in Manitou, Manitoba. There, Nellie lived with Reverend James McClung and his wife, Annie. Nellie and Annie became good friends. Annie introduced Nellie to the Women's Christian **Temperance** Union. This was a religious group concerned with the problem of alcohol abuse. Nellie enjoyed working for the group. It was the beginning of her career as an activist.

**QUICK FACTS**

• Nellie's full name at birth was Helen Letitia Mooney.

• Nellie was inspired by the writings of Charles Dickens.

• Nellie created the Winnipeg Political **Equality** League and the Federated Women's Institutes of Canada.

🍁 Nellie began writing stories when she moved into the home of Annie and James McClung.

The McClungs' had a son named Wesley. He was a pharmacist. In 1896, Nellie and Wesley married. Nellie quit teaching and became a mother. She and Wesley had five children. Even though Nellie had a large family, she began a new career as a writer. Her first book sold many copies. Nellie continued to write books and magazine articles. She wrote about marriage, war, raising a family, and the **suffrage** movement.

Nellie moved to Winnipeg with her family in 1911. In Winnipeg, she became more involved in her work as a writer and an activist. Nellie started to read to people from her books. She talked about issues that concerned her. Her favourite topics were temperance and women's rights.

People enjoyed Nellie's speeches. They were funny and entertaining. Nellie always spoke her opinion.

🍁 Nellie wrote for many popular Canadian magazines including *Maclean's* and *Chatelaine*.

# Thoughts from Nellie

Nellie was a writer, activist, and mother. Here are some of the things she said about her life.

**Nellie makes speeches in support of suffrage.**

"The real spirit of the suffrage movement is sympathy and interest in the other woman, and the desire to make the world a more homelike place to live in."

**Nellie is angry that women are not allowed to vote.**

"You'll hear from me again and you may not like it!"

**Nellie talks about her writing.**

"I wanted to put into words what I knew of those women who had been too busy making history to write it."

**Nellie fights old-fashioned ideas about women.**

"People still talk of womanhood as if it were a disease."

**Nellie argues that women should have the same rights as men.**

"We are not here to ask for a reform or a gift or a favour, but for a right—not for mercy, but for justice."

**Nellie raises five children.**

"It is not so much a woman's duty to bring children into the world as it is to see what sort of a world...she is bringing them into."

# Who Were the Famous Five?

Nellie is remembered as a member of the "Famous Five." These were five Canadian women who were involved in a court case that is now known as the Persons Case. The other women's names were Emily Murphy, Henrietta Muir Edwards, Irene Parlby, and Louise McKinney.

Under Canadian law, women were not considered persons and could not serve in the Senate. In 1927, the Famous Five asked the Supreme Court of Canada to decide if the word "person" in the **British North America Act** included women. The Supreme Court decided that "person" did not include women. Nellie and the others challenged this decision.

In 1929, the women went to the **Privy Council** in England. This court agreed with the Famous Five. Women were now considered "persons" who could serve in the Senate.

🍁 The Famous Five monument in Calgary, Alberta, honours Nellie and the other women who were involved in the Persons Case. It was sculpted by Barbara Paterson.

# Famous Five 101

### Emily Murphy (1868–1933)

Emily Murphy was a Canadian writer. In 1916, she became the first female judge in the **British Empire**. Some people said she should not be allowed to be a court judge. This is because at that time, women were not considered persons by law. Murphy decided she had to change this law. She contacted Nellie McClung, Henrietta Muir Edwards, Irene Parlby, and Louise McKinney. Together, the women went to court to obtain equal rights for women.

### Henrietta Muir Edwards (1849–1931)

Henrietta Muir Edwards was a successful artist. She used the money from selling her paintings to help poor people. Edwards worked with women prisoners, mothers, and children. Edwards became an expert on laws affecting women and children. Edwards did most of the legal research for the Persons Case.

### Irene Parlby (1868–1965)

Irene Parlby served as the president of the United Farm Women of Alberta. She wanted farm families to have good hospitals, clinics, and schools. Later, Parlby was elected to the Alberta government. She became the first woman **cabinet minister** in Alberta. Parlby and Nellie McClung were both members in Alberta's **legislature**. They worked together to create laws that helped women and children.

### Louise McKinney (1831–1903)

Louise McKinney was a teacher and an activist. McKinney supported temperance and women's suffrage. She thought she would have a stronger voice if she entered politics. McKinney **campaigned** in Alberta's provincial election in 1917. It was the first time Alberta women could vote or work as a member of the legislature. McKinney was elected and became the first female **legislator** in the British Empire.

### The Women's Suffrage Movement

When Nellie was a child, only men could vote or be politicians. Nellie and others argued that women should have the same rights as men. These women were called suffragists. They were active in Canada, Great Britain, the United States, and other countries. Nellie was a key figure in the women's suffrage movement in Canada. This movement started in Manitoba in the 1890s. Suffragists held meetings, wrote letters, and sent **petitions** to governments.

# Influences

Many people influenced Nellie's career in politics and writing. Nellie grew up in a religious family. She valued church, family life, and hard work. Annie McClung taught Nellie about temperance. This became an important issue in Nellie's work. Nellie and Annie believed that alcohol was damaging to women and their families. Nellie's work in the temperance movement made her more aware of the problems that women faced in Canada. She believed that women's rights should be protected under the law.

🍁 Nellie (right) sometimes worked with another suffragist named Emmeline Pankhurst (left). Emmeline led the suffrage movement in Great Britain.

Annie inspired Nellie to begin working in the suffrage movement. Nellie and other women helped change the voting laws in Manitoba and other provinces.

Nellie had a successful career as a writer. Her writing was influenced by a writer named Ella Cora Hind. Ella was a journalist who wrote for the *Manitoba Free Press*. She would often review Nellie's books before they were published. Ella helped Nellie improve her writing.

## Ella Cora Hind

Ella Cora Hind was born in Toronto in 1861. She moved to Winnipeg in 1882. Ella was well known for her writing about crops and farming. She also wrote about women's rights. Like Nellie, Ella was a suffragist. She helped start a group called the Manitoba Equal Franchise Club. This group worked hard so that women would be allowed to vote in Manitoba.

In 1901, Ella became a reporter for the *Manitoba Free Press*. At the paper, she wrote about crops and farming.

# Overcoming Obstacles

Nellie was a talented writer, speaker, and activist. She always supported ideas that she thought were right, even if people did not agree with her. Her biggest challenge was to change the way people thought about women's rights.

In Nellie's time, men ruled government, politics, and law. Most women worked in the home. Many people thought that women's suffrage would hurt families because women would not be at home caring for their children. Nellie worked hard to change people's views.

During this time, Sir Rodmond Roblin was the premier of Manitoba. He did not want women to vote. One day in 1914, Nellie led several hundred women to the Manitoba legislature to **protest**. Nellie made a speech. The premier listened, but he would not change his mind.

❦ Nellie proved that women could have successful careers and still be good mothers. Even though she raised five children, Nellie also wrote 16 books.

Two days later, the women returned to the legislature. They acted out a play. In the play, the women pretended to be politicians and **debated** if they should let men vote. Nellie acted as the premier. The crowd thought the play was funny.

People's attitudes were changing. A new government was elected in 1915. The following year, Manitoba became the first Canadian province to allow women to vote.

🍁 The legislative building where Nellie made her speech was replaced with a new legislative building in 1920.

# Achievements and Successes

Nellie achieved much success in her life. She was a successful writer. Her first book was published in 1908. It was called *Sowing Seeds in Danny*. The book sold more than 100,000 copies and became a Canadian bestseller. Many fans wanted to hear Nellie speak and read from her well-known books.

Nellie moved to Edmonton, Alberta, in 1915. There, she became more interested in politics. In 1921, Nellie was elected to be a **Member of the Legislative Assembly** (MLA) of Alberta. She was only the third woman in Canadian history to be elected as a member of a provincial assembly.

🍁 On June 11, 1938, a tablet honouring the Famous Five was placed in the Canadian Senate in Ottawa. Prime Minister William Lyon Mackenzie King presented the tablet to Nellie and the other women who had worked on the Persons Case.

In 1935, Nellie moved to Victoria, British Columbia. The following year, she became a **governor** of the Canadian Broadcasting Corporation (CBC). This is Canada's national radio and television broadcaster. In 1938, Nellie represented Canada at the League of Nations, an organization that promoted world peace.

Nellie lived to the age of 77. Today, Canadians remember her as someone who worked hard to ensure that women had the same rights as men.

### The Famous 5 Foundation

The Famous 5 Foundation formed in 1996. It is a charity that honours the Famous Five and other Canadian women. The foundation has installed monuments of the Famous Five in Calgary, Alberta's Olympic Plaza and on Parliament Hill in Ottawa, Ontario. Information about the five women of the Famous 5 can be found online. Visit the Famous 5 Foundation website at www.famous5.ca

In 2004, Canadians chose Nellie McClung as one of the greatest Canadians of all time in a contest held by the CBC.

# Write a Biography

A person's life story can be the subject of a book. This kind of book is called a biography. Biographies describe the lives of remarkable people, such as those who have achieved great success or have done important things to help others. These people may be alive today, or they may have lived many years ago. Reading a biography can help you learn more about a remarkable person.

At school, you might be asked to write a biography. First, decide who you want to write about. You can choose an activist, such as Nellie McClung, or any other person you find interesting. Then, find out if your library has any books about this person. Learn as much as you can about him or her. Write down the key events in this person's life. What was this person's childhood like? What has he or she accomplished? What are his or her goals? What makes this person special or unusual?

A concept web is a useful research tool. Read the questions in the following concept web. Answer the questions in your notebook. Your answers will help you write your biography.

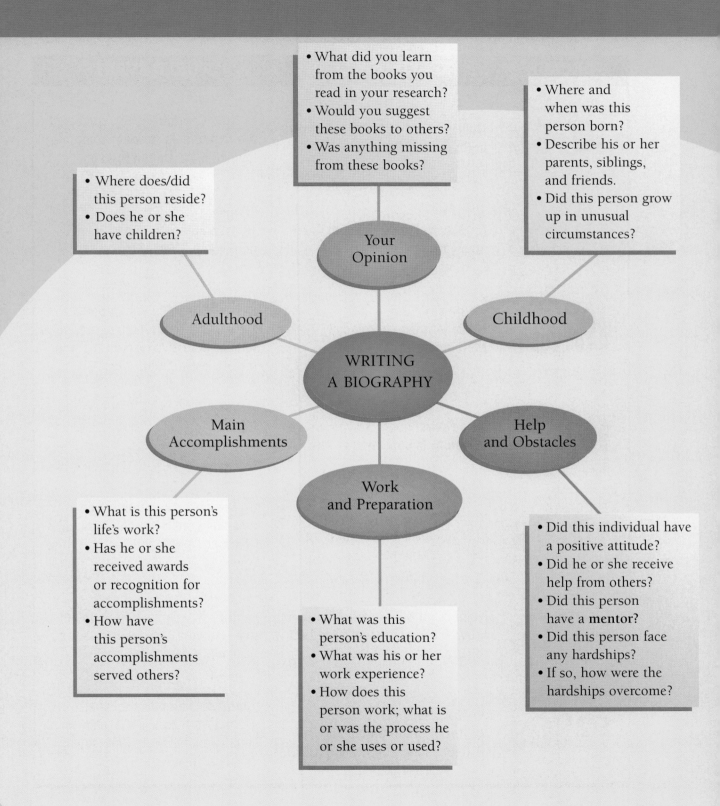

- What did you learn from the books you read in your research?
- Would you suggest these books to others?
- Was anything missing from these books?

- Where and when was this person born?
- Describe his or her parents, siblings, and friends.
- Did this person grow up in unusual circumstances?

- Where does/did this person reside?
- Does he or she have children?

**Your Opinion**

**Adulthood**

**Childhood**

**WRITING A BIOGRAPHY**

**Main Accomplishments**

**Help and Obstacles**

**Work and Preparation**

- What is this person's life's work?
- Has he or she received awards or recognition for accomplishments?
- How have this person's accomplishments served others?

- What was this person's education?
- What was his or her work experience?
- How does this person work; what is or was the process he or she uses or used?

- Did this individual have a positive attitude?
- Did he or she receive help from others?
- Did this person have a **mentor**?
- Did this person face any hardships?
- If so, how were the hardships overcome?

# Timeline

| DECADE | NELLIE MCCLUNG | WORLD EVENTS |
|---|---|---|
| **1870s** | Nellie is born on October 20, 1873, in Chatsworth, Ontario. | In 1872, Charlotte E. Ray becomes the first female African-American lawyer in the United States. |
| **1880s** | In 1880, Nellie moves with her family to Manitoba. | The Canadian Pacific Railway is completed in 1885. |
| **1890s** | Nellie marries pharmacist Wesley McClung in 1896. | In 1893, New Zealand becomes the first self-governing country in the world to give women the right to vote in elections. |
| **1900s** | Nellie's first book, *Sowing Seeds in Danny*, is published in 1908. | Queen Victoria, of Great Britain, dies in 1901. |
| **1910s** | In 1914, Nellie plays the part of Manitoba's premier in a mock parliament. | On March 3, 1913, thousands of women in the United States hold a suffrage parade outside the White House in Washington, DC. |
| **1920s** | Nellie is an MLA in the Alberta provincial government from 1921 to 1926. | In 1928, Amelia Earhart becomes the first woman to fly across the Atlantic Ocean in her airplane. |
| **1930s** | In 1936, Nellie becomes a governor of the Canadian Broadcasting Corporation (CBC). | Margaret Mitchell publishes *Gone With The Wind* in 1936. It becomes one of the best-selling books of all time. |

# Further Research

### How can I find out more about Nellie McClung?

Most libraries have computers that connect to a database for researching information. If you input a key word, you will be provided with a list of books in the library that contain information on that topic. Non-fiction books are arranged numerically, using their call number. Fiction books are organized alphabetically by the author's last name.

### Websites

To learn more about Nellie McClung, visit www.collectionscanada.ca/women, and click on "Activism" and "Nellie McClung."

To learn more about the Famous Five and the suffrage movement, visit www.abheritage.ca/famous5

# Words to Know

NEWMARKET PUBLIC LIBRARY

**activist:** a person who works for a cause

**British Empire:** colonies that were ruled by Great Britain

**British North America Act:** a document that outlined the laws of the British colonies in what is now called Canada

**cabinet minister:** an elected official who works closely with the premier on new laws

**campaigned:** gathered support for an election

**Confederation:** the creation of Canada in 1867

**debated:** argued in the government

**equality:** having the same rights as others

**governor:** a leader in an organization

**legislator:** a person who makes laws

**legislature:** the place where provincial laws are passed, also called the legislative assembly

**Member of the Legislative Assembly:** a person elected to the provincial government

**mentor:** a wise and trusted teacher

**petitions:** documents that people sign to show they support an issue

**politician:** a person who works in politics

**Privy Council:** a group of councillors appointed by the king or queen of Great Britain

**protest:** to object to something

**senate:** the upper body of government that has power over the House of Commons

**suffrage:** the right to vote in an election

**temperance:** a movement to ban the use of alcohol

**traditional:** based on long-held customs or beliefs

# Index

NEWMARKET PUBLIC LIBRARY